PICASSO

Elizabeth Elias Kaufman

CASTLE BOOKS

A Division of
BOOK SALES, INC.
110 Enterprise Avenue
Secaucus, N.J. 07094

ISBN: 0-89009-359-8

8136

CONTENTS

COLOR ILLUSTRATIONS

PABLO PICASSO

Pablo Picasso, artist, rebel, and innovator was the driving force behind twentieth century art. He was also one of the most prolific artists of all time. His skill was so great, his talent so exceptional, that there was little that anyone could teach him. Like all Spanish artists, the artistic heritage of Spain was an important part of him. However, unlike most Spanish artists, he was more of an influencer than a follower. Whatever he learned, whatever he borrowed was absorbed, analyzed, and changed to suit his artistic purposes.

He was, without a doubt, the greatest artist (and certainly the most famous) of the twentieth century. To understand Picasso's work and his place in the world of art, it is important to examine the art of the nineteenth and twentieth centuries.

HIS TIMES

To understand the relationship between art and the general cultural climate, it is only necessary to remember the change that occurred during the Renaissance. The Middle Ages stifled thinking as well as artistic creativity. There were no questions to ask; consequently, there was no searching for answers. However, the Renaissance brought a renewed interest in philosophy and learning. At the same time, the artists of the Renaissance searched for new ways to express their ideas. In this same manner, the art of the nineteenth and twentieth centuries constitutes an accurate reflection of the rapidly changing world in which it was created.

During the latter part of the nineteenth century and the early part of the twentieth century, the world of art was caught up in the throes of a number of different movements: Romanticism, Realism, Impressionism, Post-Impressionism, Expressionism, and Fauvism. Each movement was a reaction to the one that preceded it. The most important aspect of these movements is the concept that underlies them. Artists were seeking new ways to express themselves, new ways to illustrate what they saw, and new ways to free themselves from traditional styles. As each new movement became accepted, artists tried to break away from it. Thus, a "new" movement was never new for long. Once it was established, it provoked a reaction. Art became a very intellectual and rebellious exercise.

The Romanticism of the early part of the nineteenth century was replaced by Realism. Led by Gustave Courbet, the Realists were the first generation of modern painters. Their art depended on their experiences. In 1863, Edouard Manet painted *Le Dejeuner sur l'Herbe* (*Luncheon on the Grass*). This is considered by many to be the first Impressionistic work. Although it is an early piece, it displays many of the characteristics usually associated with Impressionism.

The term "Impressionism" came from the title of a piece by Claude Monet, *Impression: Sunrise.* The Impressionists broke with a tradition that had started during the Renaissance. The use of chiaroscuro (the interplay of light and dark) was more or less abandoned in favor of color and light. The shadows found in these works are usually created by using deeper colors instead of browns and blacks. There are few details, and the use of lines is kept to a minimum.

Impressionism stressed visual reality. Many of the works belonging to this period are landscapes which make no deep statement. The characterisic that is most prominent, the short brushstroke, was partially the result of an attempt to finish the work quickly before the light shifted and changed the visual experience.

The last two decades of the nineteenth century belonged to the Post-Impressionists. This somewhat nebulous term covers a large variety of styles. The two characteristics artists of this period had in common were an attempt to solidify the structures used in their art and a continued interest in light and color. Towards the end of this period, Expressionism appeared. Expressionists emphasized emotion and the human condition. Expressionism was followed by Fauvism. The artists of this school used primitive lines and forms.

By the turn of the century, art was almost totally devoid of realistic images. Realism was no longer important or even desirable. This lack of realism in art paralleled the uncertainty of life in general. The artists of the period, in their concern for ideas and concepts, were not interested in realistic portrayals.

At this time, artists from all over the world flocked to Paris. It was a magnet for them in the same way that New York has become the world capital of art today. Thus, an artist could absorb art from many different countries and cultures in Paris. There was a tremendous interest in non-European art. African sculpture, medieval art, and Oriental works were discovered, or more properly, rediscovered at this time.

As is the case with all artists, Picasso was influenced by the trends and styles. However, although he spent most of his life in other countries, Picasso was very much a product of Spain. In both his artistic work and in his private life, he exhibited the fierce individualism, independence, hardiness, and intensity that is usually associated with the Spanish character. On the other hand, Picasso always had a sense of humor and wit, characteristics seldom found in Spanish art. While Picasso was subject to many influences in the beginning and in fact throughout his career, Spain herself exerted a tremendous influence. Unlike most other Spanish artists, Picasso's art developed to the point that it was truly international. Nevertheless, the bedrock of his art and personality was Spain.

This Spanish influence is most evident in his many bull and bullfighting scenes. Other influences are not so obvious. Gertrude Stein, a lifelong friend, and one of the first people to recognize his talents, felt that Cubism was a result of his Spanish background. It is true that elements of Cubism first appeared in Picasso's work after a trip from Paris back to his home in Spain.

Given that he was influenced by his heritage, by other artists, and by art movements, it is still true that his art is unique. Very early in his career he became an innovator. During more than seventy-five years of artistic achievement, his styles and themes blend, merge, and disappear only to reappear. There are few sharp, distinct periods after his early work. Although his art may be more difficult to understand, he was as much a genius as Michelangelo or Leonardo da Vinci.

HIS LIFE

Pablo Picasso was born on October 25, 1881. He was the first child of José Ruiz Blasco and Maria Picasso Lopez. At the beginning of his career, he signed his work "Ruiz Picasso". Later, however, he dropped his father's name and used only "Picasso".

His father was a painter and art teacher. It is tempting to say that Picasso's artistic talent was inherited, but his father was not a particularly gifted artist. It is, however, safe to say that growing up in an artist's home sensitized Picasso, provided him with an opportunity to watch an artist, and allowed him to experiment with an artist's tools.

From childhood, Picasso was a strong-willed individual. His lack of interest in school resulted in poor grades. He learned early how to manipulate his parents to get his own way. His inability to tolerate rules and regulations and his total unwillingness to accept any kind of authority were traits he carried throughout his life.

Picasso began to draw almost as soon as he could hold a drawing instrument. His first oil painting was created when he was nine years old. That painting was an indication of one of his enduring passions: bullfighting.

According to a legend, the master painter Verrocchio laid down his brush and never painted again after he saw the work of his young apprentice, Leonardo da Vinci. In that same tradition, it is said that Picasso's father gave his son his own palette and brushes. By his early teenage years, Picasso had far surpassed his father.

In 1895, the family moved to Barcelona so that Picasso's father could teach at the Fine Arts Academy (known as La Lonja). Because his father was a member of the faculty, Picasso was permitted to take the entrance test for an advanced course. One of the requirements was a drawing made of a live model. Although the perspective students were given one month to finish the task, Picasso required much less time. According to one story, he finished the drawing in one week; another story has him finishing it in one day.

By 1897, La Lonja had nothing more to teach him. His family decided that he was ready for bigger and better things. Picasso was sent to Madrid. There, he passed the entrance examination for an advanced class at the Royal Academy of San Fernando. However, he couldn't tolerate the formal training. Skipping most of his classes, Picasso haunted the Prado. He was obviously very impressed with El Greco's work; because his art at the time (and later during his Blue Period) shows the same elongation and emotional tone for which El Greco was famous.

Picasso caught scarlet fever in the spring of 1898. Instead of returning to Barcelona, he went to a village in Catalonia to regain his health. There he first experienced rural life. It was a happy experience. He worked along with the villagers, taking time to sketch them.

When he returned to Barcelona, he became quite popular at a café called "Els Quatre Gats" (The Four Cats). The group of artists and intellectuals who frequented the café were rebels with a social conscience. It was at Els Quatre Gats that Picasso held his first exhibition. **By Lamplight** (plate 1) is fairly typical of his work at the time.

In 1900, Picasso and a friend decided to go to London. On the way they stopped in Paris. So intrigued were they, that they never got to London. For the next three years, Picasso shuttled back and forth between Barcelona and Paris.

Picasso's Blue Period is usually considered to have lasted from 1901 until 1904. It takes its name from the predominance of that color found in the work during the period. The paintings, all of them in near monochrome, tend to be moody, gloomy, and tragic. They are slices of life, but not happy ones.

The art he produced in 1905 and 1906 showed a marked change in style. This is considered his Rose Period. Many of the subjects are circus performers: acrobats, harlequins, and ballerinas. A delicate shade of pink is often found in the work. While not terribly happy paintings, these works are not hopeless, as was the case with the Blue Period works.

It was about this time that he met Fernande Olivier in Paris. Soon after the first meeting, she moved into his apartment as his mistress. She is often credited with helping inspire and sustain Picasso's Rose Period.

In 1907, after spending some time in Spain with Fernande, Picasso created what is recognized as the first Cubist painting, *Les Demoiselles d'Avignon* (*The Young Ladies of Avignon*). He worked on countless sketches (plate 8) before beginning the actual painting. The title refers to a street in Paris.

It is almost impossible to understand the commotion this work created. Despite the fact that Picasso was recognized as an important artist, his friends, other artists, and art dealers denounced it. Even the Fauves were stunned by it. In fact, *Les Demoiselles d'Avignon* was almost universally rejected. However, as so often happens in art, the extreme reaction stirred up interest in the style. Picasso was unperturbed by the criticism and continued working in his new style. Soon, Cubism was an accepted movement in art.

Picasso and his colleagues developed several different types or phases of Cubism including Analytical, Facet, and Collage Cubism. During part of this period, Picasso worked with the great French painter, Georges Braque (1882-1963). So close was the collaboration that is often difficult to tell which artist created which piece.

While working on Collage Cubism, Picasso was also working on another style. In the middle of Cubism, Picasso developed a style very similar to the Renaissance and Neoclassic styles. Many of the pieces showed a mother and child, such as *La Toilette* (plate 22). This ability to work in more than one style and to do so without effort was characteristic of Picasso.

His trip to Italy in 1917 may have been the spark for this new trend. Picasso, along with the painter Cocteau and the composer Satie, designed and composed a new work (called "Parade") for the Russian ballet.

On this trip, Picasso met Olga Khokhlova, one of the Russian ballerinas. In July of 1918, they were married. This was the third woman who played an important role in his life. Picasso's relationship with Fernande had ended in 1911. Shortly after that, Marcelle Humbert (whom he referred to as "Eva") moved in with him. Eva died a few years before Picasso met Olga. His relationship with women was an important part of his life and his art. Each new woman seemed to bring new inspiration. After Olga came Marie-Thérèse Walter, then Dora Maar, Françoise Gilot, and finally Jacqueline Roque.

Throughout his lifetime, Picasso continued the independent, rebellious, restless lifestyle of his youth. Never content to rest on his achievements, he ventured into the graphic arts, sculpture, and ceramics. Although he became financially secure while still fairly young, he was not interested in opulent living. He was often criticized for his Communistic politics. Through the years, his art was praised and condemned, but never ignored. Despite all the controversy, his death on April 9, 1973 left a void in the art world. He died as he had lived. He left no will; his legitimate children and illegitimate children fought over his estate. In the final analysis, what he left them is nothing when compared with what he bequeathed to the rest of the art-loving world.

HIS WORKS

PLATE 1

By Lamplight was painted in 1898. Picasso had returned from Barcelona after recuperating from scarlet fever. Picasso had recently been in Madrid where he had seen many of El Greco's works. Although the elongation does show El Greco's influence, Picasso made the style his own. His use of chiaroscuro (the interplay of light and dark) is exceptional in this piece. Notice that he was still signing his name "P. Ruiz Picasso" (bottom, right-hand corner).

At the time he painted *By Lamplight*, Picasso was only seventeen years old and had already exhibited and won a prize at the Madrid Fine Arts Exhibition.

PLATE 2

In 1901, immediately before his Blue Period, Picasso painted this *Still Life.* In it are traces of Cézanne. There is also a definite Impressionistic feel to it. The short brushstrokes and almost total lack of shadows give it a flat, two-dimensional character. It is interesting to compare this painting with later still life works such as *Still Life with Playing Cards* (plate 21), painted about eighteen years later, and with *Still Life with Owl and Mirror* (plate 40), painted forty-four years later. This comparison shows his changing styles. However, it also illustrates his propensity to return to certain subjects.

PLATE 3

The Absinthe Drinker, painted in 1903, belongs to Picasso's Blue Period. This period was partially the result of the suicide of his good friend Carles Casagemas. During this period, he painted almost no landscapes or still lifes. He was interested in people and the human condition. Many of the subjects represent the hopeless dregs of society. Although Picasso always showed compassion for his subjects, this period is probably his most compassionate and humane.

Most of the elements characteristic of the Blue Period are present in *The Absinthe Drinker:* the predominance of blue, the melancholy tone, the solitary subject, the sense of hopelessness, and the El Greco-like elongation of the figures.

PLATE 4

Picasso's Rose Period can be traced to several events. Two of the most important were his love for Fernande and the financial success he began to have. This *Mother and Child,* painted in 1905, shows the pink or "rose" color that is found in many of the works from the period. The mood had shifted from that of the preceding Blue Period. While the figures were still melancholy, there was no despair. The young boy's costume indicates he is a member of the circus. Harlequins and circus performers (especially acrobats)

were Picasso's favorite subjects during his Rose Period.

PLATE 5

In 1905, Picasso and Fernande spent a great deal of time going to the circus. In fact, he enjoyed the circus almost as much as he enjoyed bullfighting. He was there so often that he met many of the performers of the Médrano Circus.

The *Family of Acrobats with Ape* is painted in the delicate pastel shades Picasso preferred in his Rose Period. The theme of a mother and her child is one that Picasso came back to several times in his career. His love for children is obvious in each of these works. Here, he makes the child the focal point of the piece. Both the parents and the ape are watching the child.

Notice that although the hopelessness of the Blue Period had disappeared, the Rose Period was still serious and contemplative.

PLATE 6

The *Family of Saltimbanques* is often thought of as the culmination of Picasso's Rose Period. It is a strange picture. Nothing is happening; there is no internal dialogue. The characters are standing in an unidentified setting. The lower right-hand corner of the picture is occupied by a seated woman who appears to be totally unrelated to the circus family. She is not even looking at them. The other characters had been frequent subjects in his Rose Period. The acrobats, young ballerina, fat Jester, and Harlequin appeared alone and in combinations throughout the period.

One possible interpretation is that this was Picasso's final picture using these three characters. He has dressed them in such a way as to suggest that the final performance had been completed. The young ballerina wears only one slipper; the Harlequin wears a towel around his neck as does the youngest acrobat.

Both the Jester and the older acrobat appear to be carrying equipment. Several members of the family gaze towards the mysterious woman. Perhaps for Picasso, she represented a new style.

PLATE 7

This **Nude with Crossed Hands** is thought to be based on Picasso's mistress, Fernande Olivier. The piece is interesting because it was created at a juncture in Picasso's career. He was finishing his Rose Period. Within two years, he would have begun to develop Cubism.

It is a fairly realistic portrayal. However, with his usual ability to say several things at the same time, he has given the women both a sensuality and a sense of innocence.

PLATE 8

Picasso is considered to be the father of Cubism. His first Cubist piece, **Les Demoiselles d'Avignon** was finished in 1907. He executed many sketches in preparation for the piece. Originally, there were seven figures, including two males. In the final version, there are only five woman. In this **Sketch for Les Demoiselles d'Avignon,** one can see the planning involved in the final work.

With **Les Demoiselles d'Avignon,** Picasso created something new in art. The difficulty in evolving a new style is evident here. Picasso was working on the use of angles and shapes. The influence of African masks is obvious in the face, the most complete part of the sketch.

Picasso gave birth to a new way of illustrating spatial relationships. Cubism stressed the simplification of form, retaining only essential details. Like sculpture, Cubism was more interested in mass and volume than in light and atmosphere.

PLATE 9

Standing Nude is another early Cubist work. The painting shows the influence of African art. It also shows the influence of ancient Spanish sculpture. In contrast with later Cubist works, **Standing Nude** is still easily identifiable as a figure. The planes and angles have not been jumbled or rearranged. The colors are still warm and vibrant. However, most of the details have been omitted. Attention is focused on the massive, sensuous figure and her angular face. In later Cubist works, all of these characteristics disappear.

PLATE 10

In 1908, Picasso painted **Woman with a Fan.** By this time, the bright colors of **Standing Nude** (plate 9) had been replaced by dark earthy colors. Picasso did not want color to interfere in his attempt to build up volume and mass. There is a sculptural feel in this piece. It is especially obvious in the face. The woman's nose appears to have been carved from a block of wood. The only detail is the fan the woman is holding. It is the most realistic part of the work.

PLATE 11

Grand Dryad, painted in 1908, is the first of his Cubist paintings to use a landscape as part of the picture. Here, he has molded and formed the trees in the same way he has molded the woman's figure. Notice that the line of the woman's left arm is also the line of the lower part of a tree. Like the woman, the trees have a sculptural quality. The trees have been drawn to form an arch above the woman's head, framing her upper torso. Her face is a combination of the simplified face used in **Woman with a Fan** (plate 10) and the African mask used in **Standing Nude** (plate 9).

PLATE 12

The painting, *Three Women,* is an example of the importance of geometry in Cubism. Although this is a fairly early Cubist piece, already Picasso had begun to break up figures into geometric or architectural blocks. This piece is very reminiscent of some of Michelangelo's unfinished Slave sculptures. The figures appear to be trying to pull themselves free from the canvas. Picasso deliberately left the three figures in different stages of completion. The middle figure is the least complete. It looks as if a sculptor had made preliminary carvings, but had left the details for later.

PLATE 13

Nude Seated Woman presents the viewer with an unusual perspective. In the lower half of the painting, the artist appears to have been on the same level as his subject. However, in the upper half, it seems as if the artist were on a considerably lower level, looking up. In Cubism, this distortion of reality represents the way the artist sees his subject in his own mind. The sculptural quality in *Nude Seated Woman* is most clearly evident in the woman's chin. It appears as if the artist used an axe to cut out a triangular wedge.

PLATE 14

By the summer of 1909, Picasso was ready to start a new phase of Cubism. This phase is usually referred to as Analytical Cubism. The artist analyzes the parts of his subject in his mind's eye. The mind sees an entire object at once, rather than only one side. Thus, the artist's perspective is not limited to what his eye sees.

Factory in Horta was painted as a result of a summer spent at Horta de Ebro in Spain.

The piece is primarily composed of geometric blocks fitted together. Even the clouds in the background are painted as rectangles. The one exception is the treatment of the palm trees.

PLATES 15, 16, 17

The next phase of Cubism is often called Facet Cubism. *Pipes, Cup, Coffee Pot* (plate 15), *L'Independent* (plate 16), and *Man with Mandolin* (plate 17) are good examples of this phase in Cubism.

Working in close collaboration with Georges Braque, Picasso began to break his subjects into small pieces or facets. The pieces, often resembling prisms, were rearranged to suit the internal vision of the artist. For the viewer, this meant that the subject itself often disappeared. These three pieces are indicative of the lack of color in works from this period. The intent was to force the viewer to concentrate on the forms, undisturbed by color. In order to assist the viewer, signs and symbols were added. Shortly afterwards, words were added. Both *Pipes, Cup, Coffee Pot* and *L'Independent* contain printed words. The addition of words was a prelude to the next phase, Collage Cubism.

The working relationship between Picasso and Braque was close enough for them to jokingly refer to it as a marriage. So similar was the work the two men produced at the time, that in later years, they sometimes had trouble deciding who had created which unsigned piece.

PLATE 18

Collage Cubism had two stages. In the first stage, actual or simulated materials were pasted onto paper or canvas. In the second stage, the artist painted his picture to look as if materials had been pasted on instead of having been painted on.

Bouteille, Verre, & Violon (Bottle, Glass, & Violin) was created in 1913. It is an example of the first stage of Collage Cubism. Picasso cut out part of a newspaper to form the bottle on the left. The glass and other parts are also from a newspaper. Part of the violin was composed of paper, printed with a fake grain. To his pasted-on materials, Picasso added a few disciplined shapes using charcoal.

PLATE 19

Guitar, Mask, Newspaper represents the second stage of Collage Cubism. In the first stage, materials were pasted onto the paper or canvas. In the second stage, Picasso painted objects to make them seem as if they had been pasted on. Notice that the mask appears to have been pasted over a piece of the "Journal". In *Bouteille, Verre, & Violon* (plate 18), an actual piece of newsprint with the word was used. Here, Picasso uses only paint to achieve a similar effect.

In Collage Cubism, Picasso began to return to more realistic shapes. He also started using colors again. Although his palette is limited in this painting, there is more color here than in Facet Cubism as seen in *Pipes, Cup, Coffee Pot* (plate 15), *L'Independent* (plate 16), and *Man with Mandolin* (plate 17).

PLATE 20

The painting known as *Woman with a Book* shows another phase of Picasso's work in Cubism. Color reappears as an important element. However, the color is not intended to be realistic. For example, Picasso has used bright yellow stripes alternating with black to represent the woman's hair on her left side. On her right side, her hair is lavender and black. The book she holds in her hand has black printing on one page and white printing on the other page.

PLATE 21

This piece, *Still Life with Playing Cards* was painted during 1918-19. There are definite elements of Collage Cubism in it. The cards appear to have been stacked one on top of the other. An interesting part of this work is the triple frame Picasso used. In essence, it is a picture within a picture. However, even the frame appears to be a collage. On the left-hand side, one of the cards overlaps the painted frame. The cards themselves seem to be imposed on a stylized landscape. The bottom half of the painting represents some sort of ground; the upper half (especially the upper left-hand corner) shows a cloudy sky.

PLATE 22

La Toilette, painted in 1921, represents a startling departure from Cubism. During the early part of the 1920's, Picasso moved back and forth between different styles. *La Toilette* is one of a number of paintings that belong to Picasso's "classical" period. These works were created after his trip to Rome. They are generally thought to have been influenced by the classical art of Greece and Rome he saw on his trip.

One of the characteristics of this style is the heavy, sculptural quality Picasso gave to the human form. The primary figure in *La Toilette* is massive, much larger than life.

PLATE 23

One year after painting *La Toilette* (plate 22), Picasso created *Mandolin on a Table*. In this piece, he returned to his work on Cubism. Although the shape of the instrument is visible, it is disjointed and flat, and seen from several different angles. The shapes look as if they have been pasted onto the canvas. The table is treated in a similar fashion; it has no depth. The painting is beautifully balanced. The lines that represent the strings encase squares and are in turn surrounded by circles and ovals.

PLATE 24

In addition to the "classical" pictures and the return to Cubism during the 1920's, Picasso also produced a number of paintings that illustrate his continued interest in the circus and the ballet. *Harlequin with a Mirror* employs one of his favorite characters from his Rose Period. However, this figure is fuller, more robust than his earlier work. In fact, it has much in common with *La Toilette* (plate 22). Both paintings display fairly realistic forms, and in both there is a careful treatment of drapery.

PLATE 25

With *Mandolin and Music Stand*, Picasso returned once again to Cubism. The flatness of the work has the same built-up quality found in his Collage Cubism pieces. The ability to paint in several different styles at the same time is characteristic of Picasso. It is one of the hallmarks of a great and versatile artist. At the time, however, it was misunderstood. Picasso was severely criticized by other artists for having forsaken and betrayed Cubism. Art critics disliked his shifting styles; because it made it difficult to label him. Unperturbed by the furor that swirled around him and his art, Picasso continued to paint as he wanted in whatever style suited his mood.

PLATE 26

The *Greek Woman* appears to be a compromise between *La Toilette* (plate 22) and *Harlequin with a Mirror* (plate 24). The woman has less of the monumental quality than the woman in *La Toilette;* yet she has

even more of the feel of having been sculpted rather than painted. Her expression and the colors are much like *Harlequin with a Mirror.* All three works are at odds with Picasso's Cubist works of the same period.

Picasso's wit is evident in the bottom of the painting. The fairly realistic portrayal stops at the hem of the woman's dress: her feet are unfinished. Without feet, she seems to float. At the same time, her bulk appears to force her into the floor.

PLATE 27

The classical bust sitting on the table in *The Drawing Lesson* reappears in slightly different form several times in Picasso's etchings and engravings. The young boy in the painting could be his son Paul who was approximately four years old when the work was created.

In this piece, Picasso began the disintegration of the human form that appears in his later works. The face here is presented in several angles. Notice that the bust is painted in profile and full-face. The boy's face is seen almost head-on and viewed from above. As was true of all Picasso's work involving children, the boy was treated tenderly. There is an element of humor in his attempt to draw the three pieces of fruit.

PLATE 28

Musical Instruments on a Table repeats a theme Picasco used quite often at this time. Like *Mandolin and Music Stand* (plate 25), and *Mandolin on a Table* (plate 23), this piece employs musical instruments against a flat object. The composition of this painting is much freer than that of *Mandolin on a Table.* The lines seem to be etched or scratched into the canvas rather than painted. Although the painting is still flat, the objects have a lighter feel. Instead of being pasted down, they appear to float, one on top of the other.

PLATE 29

Although their intense collaboration had ended before *Fruit Dish, Bottle, Guitar* was painted, this piece does resemble some of Georges Braque's work. The objects are distorted, but still recognizable. The light background on which the objects float provides the perfect counterbalance for the heaviness of the objects. The darker background around the lighter tones emphasizes the objects and ties the painting together. It also give the piece the impression of being a painting within a painting.

PLATE 30

The title and theme of *Harlequin* is similar to work Picasso had created during his Rose Period. However, the work itself is totally different. All traces of realism have disappeared. The eyes have been scattered; the nose appears in several forms. As would be the case with a photograph, the painting seems to have both a positive and a negative image.

PLATE 31

Picasso was never really part of the Surrealism movement. However, elements of the style do appear in his work. *Woman's Head and Self-Portrait,* created in 1929, illustrates the dream-like fantasy that might emerge from the unconscious mind.

The woman's head overlaps Picasso's profile. The violence of her head is accentuated by the multiple angles from which she is viewed and by the contrast with the simplified and passive profile. At this time, Picasso was having marital problems. *Woman's Head and Self-Portrait* could represent his feelings about Olga and their marriage.

PLATE 32

By 1932, Picasso had a new mistress. Under her influence, the violent women such as was seen in *Woman's Head and Self-Portrait* (plate 31) disappeared. She was replaced by his "new" woman. *Nude in a Black Armchair* is fairly typical of this new woman. Marie-Thérèse Walter had blond hair, fair skin, and a full-bodied figure. Most of the women in this period have her hair color and skin tones. They are also rounded and very sensual.

PLATE 33

Seated Woman was painted in 1932. Like *Nude in a Black Armchair* (plate 32), it shows the influences of Picasso's new mistress. Her face is seen as a double image. One eye is facing the viewer; one is in profile. The painting has a contemplative quality that is also mysterious. Notice that in contrast with some of his earlier works, both *Seated Woman* and *Nude in a Black Armchair* are based on soft curves rather than angles and lines.

PLATE 34

Throughout his career, Picasso painted, sculpted, and etched bulls and bullfighting scenes. The *Dying Bull* shows the animal in agony. The painting provides a good contrast with a sculpture Picasso created nine years later in 1943. The *Bull's Head* was made with the seat of a bicycle and a set of handlebars. The wit and whimsy of the sculpture is missing in this painting. The fierceness of the open mouth is similar in feel to the woman's mouth in *Woman's Head and Self-Portrait* (plate 31) painted in 1932.

PLATE 35

Thirty-six years before he painted *Woman Reading,* Picasso had painted *By Lamplight* (plate 1). A comparison of the two pieces is quite interesting. In the earlier work, the artist was working on the effects of light. The lamp on the table plays a major role in the painting. In the later work, the lamp is only a prop. Other elements that can be compared are the tables, the hands of the two figures, and the chairs. It is difficult to believe that one artist created both paintings.

PLATE 36

Still Life with Coffee Pot was painted in 1936. Notice that the piece is carefully balanced. The many sharp angles are played against arcs and circles. The colors are also very well balanced. The heavy use of black is countered with red, yellow, and pastel shades.

PLATE 37

Picasso often painted portraits of the women in his life. This *Portrait of Dora Maar* was painted in 1939. Although there are the proper number of features (Picasso often gave his portraits more than one set of features), the face is disjointed and very asymmetrical. The painting seems to suggest that the artist saw two women in Dora Maar's face. Even the hair color is split. On the left-hand side, her hair is first black, then red; on the right-hand side, it is first red, then black. Two years later, in 1941, Picasso painted her portrait again (plate 39). In the second portrait, her face is even more disjointed.

PLATE 38

One of the themes that runs through Picasso's work is the seated female. *Woman in an Armchair* was painted in 1941. It makes an interesting contrast to *Nude in a Black Armchair* (plate 32). This painting is much more angular. Unlike *Nude in a Black Armchair,* it is based on lines and angles, rather than curves and circles.

As was the case with both of the Dora Maar portraits (plates 37, 39), the face is seen from a variety of angles. In fact, the model for this piece was probably Dora Maar.

PLATE 39

This *Portrait of Dora Maar,* painted in 1941, is almost primitive when compared with the earlier portrait (plate 37) painted in 1939. Here, the artist has almost disconnected the two sides of her face. The rough surface quality and the heavy emphasis on angles might reflect the problems in their relationship.

In both *Woman in an Armchair* (plate 38) and this portrait, Picasso gave the woman a hat. The hat on the *Woman in an Armchair* is fanciful and humorous. The hat in this painting is as primitive and even childish as the rest of the painting.

PLATE 40

Under the influence of Françoise Gilot, the new woman in his life, Picasso's style shifted slightly again. In *Still Life with Owl and Mirror,* painted in 1945, Picasso relied on lines. Instead of being dominated by curves and angles, the line itself is the controlling factor here.

PLATE 41

La Joie de Vivre was painted in 1946 in Antibes. This was a very happy time in Picasso's life. The war was over, and he had a new love, Françoise Gilot. The painting reflects his joy. On the left, a faun is playing a flute. On the right, a satyr is playing another instrument. Between them, a woman and two goats are dancing. In the upper left-hand corner, there is a sailboat, emphasizing the seaside motif. The woman is usually thought to represent Françoise. Picasso often painted her figure as a flower-like shape. The entire composition is bright and airy.

PLATE 42

Early in 1955, Picasso moved into a villa in Cannes. The *Studio, Cannes* was painted that same year. Evidently, Picasso enjoyed working in his new home. The painting shows a bright and sunny room. The height of the ceiling was emphasized by the dimensions of the canvas he used - the height is more than twice the size of the width. This is an intimate glimpse into the cluttered environment in which Picasso worked.

PLATE 43

Beginning in 1945, Picasso worked in lithography. *Buste de Femme* was created more than ten years after he started this new work. Incorporated in the piece is something missing from the majority of Picasso's work - a shadow. The model for the piece was probably Françoise Gilot. Although the two sides of her face are different, neither the face nor the individual features are disjointed as was the case in his portraits of Dora Maar (plates 37, 39). Each new woman in his life led to a new style. In this case, he seemed to have been very interested in details such as the beads around her neck and her elaborate costume.

PLATE 44

By 1960 when *The Arena, Arles* was executed, Picasso was deeply involved with Jacqueline Roque. A year later, they were married. As always, a new woman brought a new style. This piece could almost have been fingerpainted. Instead of concealing his brushstrokes, Picasso emphasized them. He used squiggly lines to represent rows of seats. A few curved lines of different colors define the center of the arena. Although fairly detailed, this work has the same light touch that *The Studio, Cannes* (plate 42) has.

PLATE 45

Picasso returned to a favorite theme, still life, with *Mandolin, Jug, & Glass.* A mandolin appears in many of his earlier works such as *Man with Mandolin* (plate 17), *Mandolin on a*

Table (plate 23), and *Mandolin and Music Stand* (plate 25). Apparently Picasso was fascinated with the rhythmic shape of the instrument. The lines in *Mandolin, Jug, & Glass* all follow the contours of the objects. It is as if each object radiates its own glowing shape.

PLATE 46

The boy's face in *Woman Eating a Melon and Boy Writing* shows the same concentration as in *The Drawing Lesson* (plate 27). Part of the humor of the painting is due to the way Picasso has posed both figures in awkward positions. The boy is trying to write while on his stomach, his feet dangling in the air. The woman is attempting to eat the melon while curled into a pretzel-like posture.

PLATE 47

After his marriage to Jacqueline Roque in 1961, Picasso moved to another villa. This one was located in Mougins. *Landscape at Mougins* was painted in 1965. Although full of details, the work has an elemental simplicity. It shows a peaceful, sunny village. The painting is an indication of the peace he had found with his new wife in his new home.

PLATE 48

Imaginary Portrait was created in 1969. Picasso was eighty-eight years old at the time; still productive, and still finding new ways to amuse and delight his public. Although Picasso never said anything about it, it is impossible not to see his contemporary, Salvadore Dali in the piece. The mustache and flowing hair were Dali trademarks. The title may refer to the fact that Dali never sat for the portrait. It may also be Picasso's comment on Dali's works. In any event, the piece illustrates the wit and imagination that characterized so much of Picasso's work.

Plate 1 By Lamplight, 1898, oil on canvas, 30½″ x 24½″, private collection

Plate 2 Still Life, 1901, oil on canvas, 23½″ x 31⅝″, Museum, Barcelona

Plate 3 The Absinthe Drinker, 1903, oil on canvas,
27½″ x 21¾″, private collection

Plate 4 Mother and Child, 1905, gouache on canvas,
2′ 11½″ x 2′ 6″, Staatsgalerie, Stuttgart

Plate 5 Family of Acrobats with Ape, 1905, India ink, gouache, watercolor,
and pastel on cardboard, 3′ 5″ x 2′ 5½″, Kunstmuseum, Göteborg

Plate 6 Family of Saltimbanques, 1905, oil on canvas, 6′ 11¾″ x 7′ 6⅜″,
National Gallery of Art, Washington, D. C.

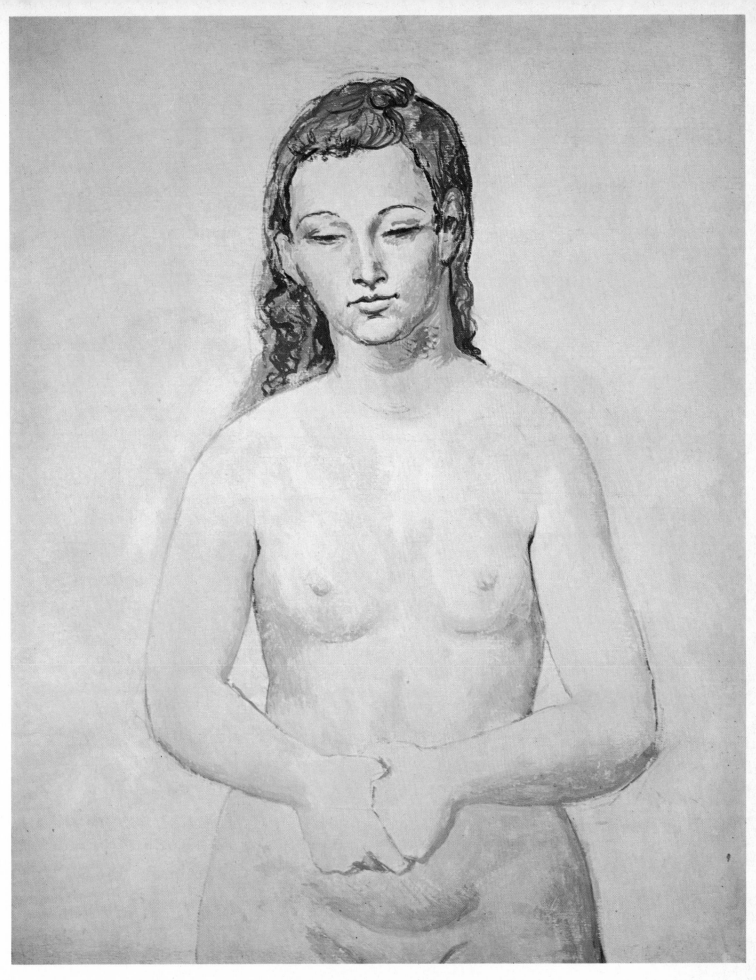

Plate 7 Nude with Crossed Hands, 1905, gouache on canvas,
3′ 1¾″ x 2′ 5¾″, Zacks, Toronto

Plate 8 Sketch for Les Demoiselles d'Avignon, 1907, oil on canvas,
30″ x 20¾″, Carlo Fruade Angeli Collection, Milan

24

Plate 9 Standing Nude, 1907, oil on canvas, 3′ ½″ x 1′ 5″, Jucker, Milan   **25**

Plate 10 Woman with a Fan, 1908, oil on canvas,
4′ 1⅝″ x 3′ 3⅜″, Hermitage, Leningrad

Plate 11 Grand Dryad, 1908, oil on canvas, 6′ 1″ x 3′ 6½″,
Hermitage, Leningrad

27

Plate 12 Three Women, 1908, oil on canvas, 5′ 10″ x 6′ 7″,
Hermitage, Leningrad

Plate 13 Nude Seated Woman, 1909, oil on canvas,
28¾″ x 23½″, private collection

29

Plate 14 Factory in Horta, 1909, oil on canvas,
20⅞″ x 23⅝″, Hermitage, Leningrad

Plate 15 Pipes, Cup, Coffee Pot, 1910, oil on canvas,
19⅞″ x 50¼″, private collection

Plate 16 L'Independent, 1911, oil on canvas, 24″ x 19¾″,
private collection

Plate 17 Man with Mandolin, 1911, oil on canvas,
24″ x 14½″, Gianni Mattioli, Milan

33

Plate 18 Bouteille, Verre, & Violon, 1913, pasted paper and
charcoal on canvas, Tzara Collection, Paris

34

Plate 19 Guitar, Mask, Newspaper, 1913, oil on canvas,
24″ x 17″, Masurel, Roubaix

36   **Plate 20 Woman with a Book,** 1917-18, oil on canvas, private collection

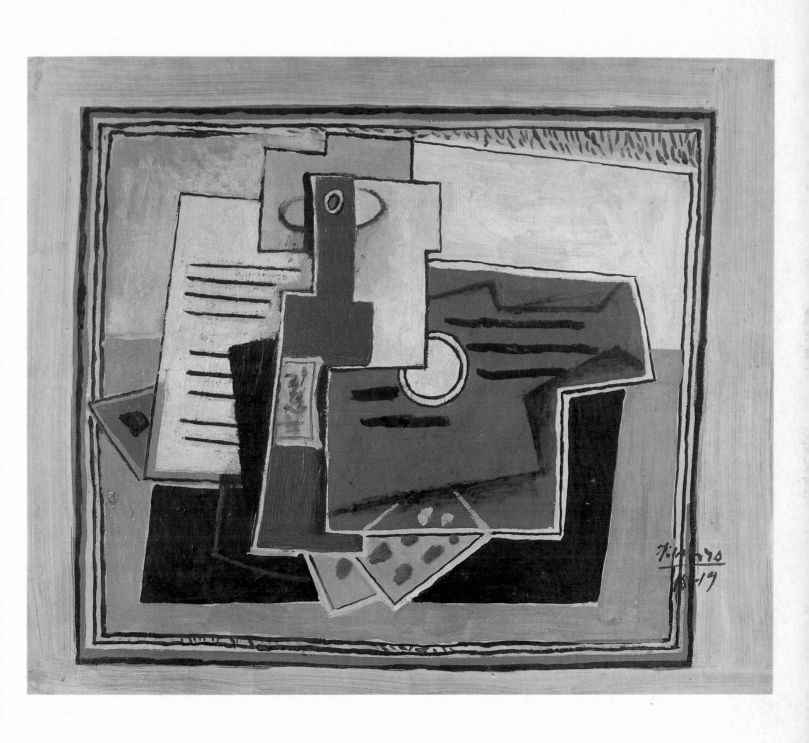

Plate 21 Still Life with Playing Cards, 1918-19, oil on canvas,
25½″ x 21″, Galerie Rosengart, Lucerne

Plate 22 La Toilette, 1921, oil on canvas, 8¾″ x 6¼″,
private collection

Plate 23 Mandolin on a Table, 1922, oil on canvas,
2′ 8″ x 3′ 3½″, private collection

Plate 24 Harlequin with a Mirror, 1923, oil on canvas,
3′ 3⅜″ x 2′ 7⅞″, private collection

Plate 25 Mandolin and Music Stand, 1923, oil on canvas,
3′ 2¼″ x 4′ 3¼″, private collection

Plate 26 Greek Woman, 1924, oil on canvas, 5′ 11⅝″ x 2′ 5⅛″,
Galerie de l'Elysée, Paris

Plate 27 The Drawing Lesson, 1925, oil on canvas,
4′ 3″ x 3′ 2¼″, private collection

Plate 28 Musical Instruments on a Table, 1925, oil on canvas,
6′ 1¾″ x 6′ 8½″, Galerie Bayeler, Basel

Plate 29 Fruit Dish, Bottle, Guitar, 1925, oil on canvas,
3′ 3¾″ x 5′ 1″, private collection

Plate 30 Harlequin, 1927, oil on canvas, 31¾″ x 25½″,
private collection

Plate 31 Woman's Head and Self-Portrait, 1929, oil on canvas,
2′ 5″ x 2′, private collection

Plate 32 Nude in a Black Armchair, 1932, oil on canvas,
6′ 1¾″ x 4′ 3⅛″, private collection

Plate 33 Seated Woman, 1932, oil on panel,
29¼″ x 20⅝″, private collection

49

Plate 34 Dying Bull, 1934, oil on canvas, 13″ x 21½″,
private collection

Plate 35 Woman Reading, 1934, oil on canvas,
5′ 3¾″ x 4′ 3⅛″, private collection

Plate 36 Still Life with Coffee Pot, 1939, oil on canvas,
13″ x 17½″, private collection

Plate 37 Portrait of Dora Maar, 1939, oil on panel,
23½″ x 17¾″, private collection

Plate 38 Woman in an Armchair, 1941, oil on canvas, 4′ 3″ x 3′ 2″,
private collection

Plate 39 Portrait of Dora Maar, 1941, oil on canvas,
16⅛″ x 13⅛″, private collection

Plate 40 Still Life with Owl and Mirror, 1945, oil on canvas,
2′ 7⅞″ x 3′ 9½″, private collection

Plate 41 La Joie de Vivre, 1946, oil on fibro-cement panel,
3′ 11¼″ x 8′ 2½″, Musée Grimaldi, Antibes

Plate 42 The Studio, Cannes, 1955, oil on canvas,
6′ 4¼″ x 2′ 7½″, private collection

Plate 43 Buste de Femme, after Lucas Cranach the Younger,
1958, color linoleum cut, 25⅝″ x 20⅞″,
courtesy the FAR Gallery, New York

59

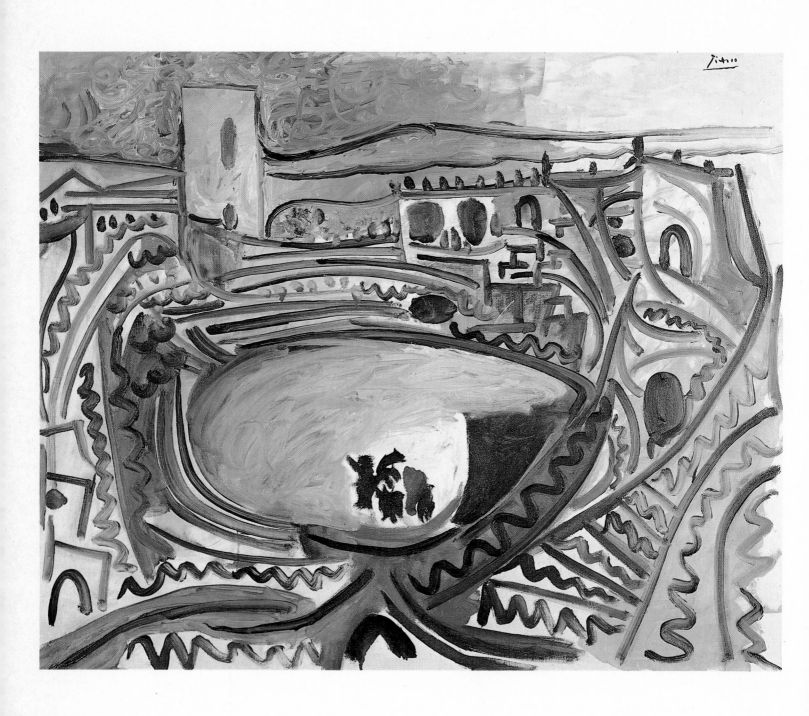

Plate 44 The Arena, Arles, 1960, oil on canvas,
2′ 8″ x 3′ 3½″, private collection

Plate 45 Mandolin, Jug, & Glass, 1962, oil on canvas,
2′ 4½″ x 3′ ⅛″, private collection

Plate 46 Woman Eating a Melon and Boy Writing, 1965,
oil on canvas, 4′ 3″ x 5′ 4″, private collection

Plate 47 Landscape at Mougins, 1965, oil on canvas,
2′ 1½″ x 3′ 3¼″, private collection

Plate 48 Imaginary Portrait, 1969, lithograph on wrapping
paper, 25⅝″ x 19⅝″